CLIENTS ACQUSITION AND RETENTION:
TECHNIQUES TO PROPEL YOUR LAW FIRM
TOWARDS SUCCESS.

CLIENTS ACQUISITION AND RETENTION:
TECHNIQUES TO PROPEL YOUR LAW FIRM
TOWARDS SUCCESS.

THE POCKET GUIDE FOR WINNING LAWYERS.

OLA OSHODI

ISBN:979-830-043-387-1
ISBN: 979-830-296-845-6

DEDICATION.
To my Beloved Children.
Amatul-Kafeel, Karima and Mustafa.

Table of Contents

Author's Note

There exists an unspoken expectation that upon being called to the bar, business will naturally flow to you, and clients will flock to your office. In my view, this assumption is not adequately addressed at the university which plays a pivotal role in shaping the future of legal professionals. It seems to me that a crucial component of practicing law within a firm setting is missing from the curriculum, leaving bright and eager minds unprepared for the challenges they will face in the real world.

This gap in education has led many aspiring legal luminaries to struggle through their legal practice, seek alternative sources of income, or abandon their practice altogether. Marketing is a core course that would benefit the majority of final-year law students who aspire to practice within a firm, and such course would be a significant step towards bridging the gap. It would provide students with a comprehensive understanding of how to market their services, build a client base, and maintain long-term relationships with clients regardless of their personality. This would be in addition to law firm internship and mandatory pupillage.

Marketing is not just about promoting oneself but understanding the needs of clients and providing them with the best possible service. Building a brand, establishing a reputation, and creating a network of contacts are skills that can be learned and honed through proper education and training. These skills are crucial for success in a law firm setting, where competition is fierce, and the ability to attract and retain clients can make or break a career.

The assumptions that business will come naturally to new lawyers and that they will be ready to take on the world after a few years of practice is misguided. The reality is that success in the legal profession requires a combination of legal knowledge and business acumen. Higher institutions have a responsibility to prepare students for this reality by including practical courses such as marketing in their curriculum. By doing so, they can help aspiring lawyers navigate the challenges of legal practice and achieve long-term success in their careers.

Introduction.

Success in the legal profession is much about building a strong client base as it is about practicing the law. Yet many skilled lawyers struggle to establish and maintain this essential client pipeline. To address this need, this lawyers' marketing guide outlines practical strategies to help legal professionals develop a compelling, client-focused approach to marketing their law firm and growing their law firm's business brand.

This book delves into the significance of identifiable law firm marketing objectives, which serve as the foundation for any successful client acquisition and retention strategy. By setting clear, measurable goals that align with your law firm's objectives, you will be better equipped to take actionable steps that translate to growth.

The digital landscape today provides unique opportunities to engage with potential clients. This book highlights the value of using paid online advertising to connect with your target audience on the platforms they frequent most. Maintaining a steady online presence is crucial for establishing trust and for positioning yourself and your law firm as an authority in your practice areas.

Investing in advertisement is another critical component of an effective marketing strategy. Paid advertising, whether digital or traditional, can amplify your law firm's visibility among your target audiences and accelerate your law firm's client acquisition aims. Efficient advertising campaigns allow you to highlight your distinguished services and connect with clients seeking specific expertise. Moreover, advertisements designed around your practice's unique selling points help differentiate you from competitors in the legal space thereby enhancing your overall brand.

Networking, both in person and online, is an invaluable strategy in legal marketing that should not be underestimated. Building relationships within and outside the legal community can yield long-term benefits, from direct client referrals to collaborations with other industry professionals. By actively engaging in networking opportunities, you will create a strong network that supports your client acquisition goals and solidifies your reputation within your areas of practice. In legal practice, word of mouth remains a powerful strategy, and cultivating professional relationships can be one of the most effective ways to build a solid client pipeline.

The value of mentorship is immeasurable. Finding a mentor with relevant experience in your practice areas can be profoundly beneficial both personally and professionally. Mentors can provide invaluable guidance, share their expertise, and offer support, helping you navigate the complexities of your career. A mentor's wisdom and experience can be a catalyst for your growth, enabling you to achieve your professional goals more efficiently and effectively.

Finally, this book includes an overview of essential marketing resources designed to enhance your marketing skills. By leveraging these tools, you can gain a deeper understanding of best practices, work smarter, analyze your marketing efforts effectively, and stay updated on the latest trends in legal marketing. With thoughtful planning and consistent effort, you can develop a robust marketing infrastructure that attracts clients, stimulates long-term relationships, and enables sustained growth and career success.

I.

Strategic Marketing Objectives.

A business plan is essential for the long-term growth of your law firm, as this will form the bedrock against which most strategic decisions that may impact the growth of your law firm will be made. The vision and objectives of your law firm should inspire your firm's marketing objectives, and for this reason, you should explore strategic approaches towards the acquisition and retention of clients.

Strategic marketing objectives for your law firm are essential for driving growth, building brand recognition, and establishing your firm as a forerunner in specialized legal areas. Your strategic marketing objectives should focus on attracting high-value clients, who not only contribute directly to revenue but also bring opportunities for long-term relationships and valuable referrals. Your law firm's strategic marketing objectives must also prioritize increasing your law firm's brand visibility, making your law firm more recognizable and accessible to potential clients. This can be achieved through various methods, including but not limited to targeted advertising, thought leadership, and consistent engagement across digital and traditional channels.

Furthermore, it is essential to build a reputation for expertise in specific law practice areas where your law firm can stand out. By emphasizing strengths in niche legal areas, your law firm will position itself as a trusted advisor for clients seeking specialized legal knowledge. This reputation for excellence can be fostered through publishing relevant content, participating in law events, and obtaining professional certifications.

Note that your law firm's strategic marketing objectives should be closely aligned with your law firm's broader business goals and ensure that all efforts contribute to sustainable business growth. For instance, client acquisition efforts should also consider client retention strategies, creating value and satisfaction that encourage loyalty. Also, by focusing on niche markets, your law firm can achieve a dominant position, setting itself apart from your competitors in these specialized areas. These objectives are broken down into specific categories below.

Client Onboarding

To attract new clients in targeted practice areas, your law firm should focus its marketing efforts on building awareness and credibility in these specific practice areas. Techniques such as content marketing, search engine optimization (SEO), and social media campaigns can effectively position your law firm as a trusted advisor. This strategic approach will enhance your law firm's visibility and reputation, leading to increased inquiries and consultations. By concentrating on these methods, your law firm can successfully expand its client base and establish a strong presence in the selected practice areas.

Brand Profile

The objective of having a brand profile is to establish a recognizable and reputable brand for your law firm within the legal community and target markets. To set your law firm apart from your competitors, your law firm needs strong brand visibility which can be achieved through consistent branding, including logos and messaging, demonstrating thought leadership by publishing articles and blogs, and by participating in legal summits. Purposeful networking is also crucial. Public relations efforts, such as being featured in legal publications or speaking at industry events, can further enhance your law firm's brand and reputation. By focusing on these strategies, your law firm can build a strong, credible presence that attracts clients and helps you stand out in the competitive legal landscape.

Referrals and Client Loyalty

To ensure sustainable business growth, it is essential to foster strong business relationships with existing clients and referral partners. In the legal community, where personalized service is of significant advantage, referrals are important. The client retention strategy should include regular check-ins, offering additional services at a discount, and maintaining a client newsletter with relevant legal insights. Additionally, depending on your areas of practice, engaging with other professionals, such as accountants or real estate agents, for cross-referrals is essential. This approach ensures that your law firm can build lasting relationships that drive your ongoing business and enhance your law firm's brand in the legal community.

Digital Visibility

Potential clients frequently search for legal services online and, so, it is crucial to have an optimized website that clearly communicates your legal niche areas. Investing in search engine optimization (SEO), Google ads, and local business listings can significantly enhance your law firm's visibility in online search results. Also, your website should feature user-friendly call-to-action options and easy scheduling for legal consultations. By focusing on these strategies, your law firm can attract more prospective clients and convert them into loyal clients. The objective is to optimize your law firm's online presence to generate leads and drive conversions.

Audience-Specific Marketing Campaigns

To effectively target specific legal niches, it is vital to develop and implement tailored marketing campaigns. These campaigns can be designed to reach industries, such as tech startups that require contracts or real estate brokers who require closing lawyers. Utilizing email marketing can capture the attention of your specific audience by offering solutions directly relevant to their legal needs. These marketing campaign strategies, which will be discussed in details in later sections, will ensure that your marketing efforts are both efficient and impactful in attracting and engaging clients within specific sectors, ultimately driving more inquiries and conversions.

Client Testimonials and Success Stories

Trust is paramount in the legal industry and prospective clients seek proof of experience and competence to build trust and credibility. Collecting and promoting client testimonials, reviews, and summaries of completed cases can effectively demonstrate your law firm's track record. Sharing success stories on your social media, your firm's website, and in marketing materials can be compelling and can attract new clients. By highlighting real-world examples of your law firm's achievements, you will provide tangible evidence of your legal knowledge and reliability, making your law firm more appealing to potential clients. Be sure to seek your client's consent before sharing these stories and consider requisite privacy laws and your professional responsibilities in your jurisdiction.

Expertise and Credibility

To position your law firm and the lawyers in your firm as experts in the legal field, focus on creating informative content. Hosting webinars, writing blog posts, and speaking at legal conferences can establish your law firm and its lawyers as leaders in their areas of expertise. Sharing legal updates, providing insights into industry changes, and offering free legal resources can attract attention from both potential clients and referral partners. By consistently delivering valuable information, your law firm can build and improve its brand reputation, making it a go-to resource for legal advice and services.

Networking and Strategic Collaborations

Professional relationships create business development opportunities. Depending on your chosen areas of legal practice, networking with the right professionals can generate valuable referrals. For example, a lawyer who practices real estate may potentially benefit from nurturing professional relationships with real estate brokers, real estate boards and real estate agents.

Also, a lawyer who practices tax law or corporate finance may potentially benefit from nurturing professional relationships with accountants and financial advisors. By joining industry-specific associations or attending relevant meetups and conferences, your law firm can remain a high priority for potential partners who can refer business. This strategic approach allows your law firm to maintain mutually beneficial professional relationships with various professional networks which can enhance your law firm's growth. Engaging in these activities ensures that your law firm is well positioned within the industry, leading to increased referrals and business opportunities.

Emerging Trends

To remain competitive, you should stay updated with changes in the legal industry and adapt your strategic marketing strategies accordingly. Legal marketing continuously evolves, especially with advancements in technology and shifting client expectations. Your law firm should be agile, leveraging data and market research to refine its strategies as needed. This could involve adopting new digital tools, exploring emerging practice areas, or targeting different demographics. By staying informed and flexible, your law firm can effectively respond to industry trends and client needs, ensuring sustained growth and relevance in the market.

Maximize Earnings per Client

To increase client contribution to your business revenue, consider upselling additional services or retainers to existing clients. Law firms frequently serve clients with recurring or diverse legal needs. Developing a strategy to upsell additional services that can significantly enhance the value of each client to your law firm; for example, a corporate lawyer can offer corporate record retention alongside setting up their client's business corporation which can lead to further earnings for the law firm, or propose long-term retainers that offer ongoing service and loyalty. By identifying and addressing the varied needs of your clients, you can provide comprehensive solutions that foster long-term relationships and increase client satisfaction. This approach not only boosts revenue but also strengthens client loyalty and trust in your law firm's capabilities.

Aligning marketing objectives with business goals, such as revenue growth, client retention, and market authority, ensures a comprehensive and effective marketing strategy. This alignment helps your law firm attract and retain clients while establishing a leading industry presence. By integrating these objectives, your law firm can create targeted marketing campaigns that support your overall business ambitions. This strategic marketing approach enhances client acquisition, fosters long-term business relationships, and strengthens your law firm's position in the legal market. Ultimately, a well-aligned marketing strategy drives sustainable growth and competitive advantage, ensuring your law firm's continued success in the legal industry.

II.

Optimum Client Model.

The optimum client model for your law firm can be categorized into two key frameworks: the Vertical Model, which focuses on industries or sectors, and the Horizontal Model, which considers factors such as the business size, geography, or client type. By clearly defining these models, your law firm can strategically align its marketing efforts to target and attract the most suitable clients effectively. This approach enhances your law firm's outreach and also ensures a more custom-made and impactful engagement with prospective clients, ultimately fostering stronger client relationships and driving sustainable growth for your law firm.

The Vertical Model

The Vertical Model is an approach that emphasizes serving specific industries or sectors that align with your law firm's areas of expertise. By focusing on particular industries, your law firm can align its services to meet the unique needs and challenges of those sectors, thereby enhancing its value proposition and competitive edge.

Law firms often specialize in various areas of law, such as corporate law, intellectual property, real estate, animal law, labour law, environmental law or healthcare law. The ideal clients for these specialized law firms are individuals, businesses, and organizations within industries that require those specific legal services. For example, a law firm specializing in environmental law would target clients in the government, in not-for-profit organizations, and in the oil sector, to name a few.

Implementing the Vertical Model involves implementing the following key steps:

Identify Target Industries: Determine which industries align with your law firm's areas of practice. Consider factors such as market demand, industry growth potential, and the specific legal needs of businesses within those sectors.

Develop Industry Expertise: Build a deep understanding of the legal and regulatory landscape of your target industries. This includes staying updated on industry trends, attending relevant conferences, and engaging with industry associations.

Customize Services to Industry Needs: Customize your legal services to address the specific challenges and requirements of your target industries. This may involve developing specialized practice groups or offering industry-specific legal solutions.

Market Your Expertise: Promote your law firm's industry expertise through targeted marketing efforts. This can include publishing industry-focused content, participating in industry events, and leveraging industry-specific marketing channels.

Build Relationships: Establish and nurture relationships with key stakeholders within your target industries. This includes networking with industry leaders, forming strategic partnerships, and actively engaging with industry communities.

By adopting the Vertical Model, your law firm can position itself as a trusted advisor and legal partner for businesses within your chosen industries. This focused approach enhances your law firm's brand and reputation. It also drives client acquisition and sustainable client retention.

The Horizontal Model

The Horizontal Model is a strategic approach that emphasizes the size and geographic location of clients, making them ideal for your law firm. Unlike industry-specific models, the Horizontal Model focuses on broader elements such as client size and geographic location, allowing your law firm to cater to a diverse range of clients across various sectors. This flexibility allows your law firm to adapt to changing market conditions and client needs, ensuring sustained growth and success.

Implementing the Horizontal Model involves identifying the following:

Client Size: The client size approach targets clients based on their size, whether small businesses, mid-sized companies, or large corporations. By understanding the unique needs and challenges associated with different client sizes, your law firm can adapt its services to provide the most effective legal solutions. For example, small businesses may require assistance with startup legalities and compliance, while larger corporations might need support with complex mergers and acquisitions.

Geographic Location: This approach allows your law firm to focus on specific regions or areas where there is a high demand for legal services. By concentrating on geographic locations, your law firm can build a strong local presence, develop relationships with local businesses, and gain a deeper understanding of legal issues.

It is essential to focus on the key strategies to successfully implement the Horizontal Model. Adapt your services to align with the specific demands of different business sizes, geographies, and client types. Establish a strong local presence in targeted areas to enhance visibility and accessibility for prospective clients. By adopting the Horizontal Model, your law firm can effectively expand its client base, enhance its market presence, and provide custom-made legal solutions to a diverse range of clients.

III.

Target Client Profile.

A target client profile is a detailed description of the ideal potential client for your law firm, tailored to your specific areas of practice. This profile can be divided into two categories: the industry-specific profile and the generic client profiles.

Industry-Specific Profile.

The industry-specific profile focuses on the characteristics of clients within a specific business niche that aligns with your law firm's practice areas. By identifying and understanding these characteristics, you can streamline your marketing strategy to better address the needs of these clients. Essential components to consider when developing an industry-specific profile include:

Demographics: This includes age, gender, location, and other relevant demographic information.

Industry: The specific industry or sector in which the potential client operates.

Estimated Annual Revenue: An estimate of the financial size of the potential client, which can help determine their ability to afford your services.

Predictable Goals: Common objectives and goals that clients in this niche typically pursue.

Challenges: The specific legal challenges and issues that clients in this industry face.

Legal Needs: The types of legal services that are most relevant and beneficial to clients in this niche.

Refining potential clients based on the above components will aid your law firm in structuring its marketing strategies based on your clients' distinctive needs and challenges.

Generic Client Profile

The generic client profile encompasses broader characteristics that apply to potential clients across various industries. This profile helps you identify common traits and needs among your prospective clients, regardless of their specific business niche. Key elements to consider when developing a generic client profile include:

Demographics: General demographic information that applies to a wide range of clients.

Client Size: The size of the client, whether they are individuals, small businesses, or large corporations.

Geographic Location: The regions or areas where your potential clients are located.

Engagement Preferences: How clients prefer to interact with your law firm, such as through in-person meetings, phone calls, or digital communication.

Challenges: The legal and regulatory issues that clients in this industry may face.

Common Legal Needs: Legal services that are broadly applicable and beneficial to clients in various industries.

By understanding these universal characteristics, you can create marketing strategies that appeal to a wide audience while still addressing the specific needs of individual clients.

Developing a comprehensive target client profile allows your law firm to effectively identify and attract ideal clients. By understanding the unique characteristics and needs of your potential clients, you can tailor your marketing strategies to demonstrate how your law firm can provide valuable legal solutions. This targeted approach not only enhances your law firm's ability to attract new clients but also strengthens your overall marketing efforts.

Examples of the industry-specific profile and the generic client profile are contained in the appendices of this book.

IV.

Impact Statement.

An impact statement is a compelling tool that enables you to succinctly and clearly present your services to potential clients. Given that first interactions are often the major chance you have to make a lasting impression, it is crucial to model your impact statements to suit different networking events and professional environments. When crafting your impact statement, consider it as your only opportunity to highlight your law firm and its areas of expertise.

The following practical guidelines can be useful for creating an effective impact statement to leave a great impression:

Potential Clients: Understanding what clients' need is essential to providing workable solutions. Model your message to address your potential clients' specific challenges and how your services can provide solutions.

Succinct and Clear: As a principle, you should always aim for clarity and brevity. It is best to use simple language to convey your message. Avoid ambiguous words or terms that might confuse your potential clients.

Your Law Firm's Unique Expertise: Every law firm is unique so your law firm's uniqueness should be identified in relation to your competitors. Emphasize the unique skills, experiences, and successes that make your legal services valuable.

Focus on Benefits: Rather than just listing your services, explain the benefits your clients will gain. Show how your services can improve their business, save them time, and solve their problems.

Positive Language: Choose words that convey confidence and professionalism. Positive language can create a more compelling and persuasive impact statement.

Call to Action: Encourage your targeted prospective client to take the next step, whether it is scheduling a meeting, visiting your website, or contacting you for more information.

Practice and Refine: Rehearse your impact statement until it feels natural. Be prepared to adjust it based on feedback and different networking scenarios.

By following these steps, you can create a compelling impact statement that effectively communicates the value of your services and leaves a lasting impression on potential clients. Also, you can build brand recognition, generate client leads, and foster strong business relationship with potential clients.

V.

Web Platform.

Maintaining a consistent online presence is essential for any business in this era, and there are various types of web platforms your law firm can adopt to achieve this. One of the most effective ways to establish your online presence is by creating an official website for your law firm. This website will serve as a comprehensive resource that describes the services your law firm provides. While it is important to provide a high-level overview of your services, it is equally crucial to consider the specific areas of practice within your law firm and determine whether sub-sections should be included on your official website.

When designing your website, you should include the services your law firm provides and present the lawyers who work at your law firm. Clients prefer to have a sense of who they will be interacting with, so including the professional backgrounds for members of your team will provide your website visitors with this vital information.

Also, the mission and objectives of your law firm add a personalized touch to your website, making clients feel valued and understood rather than just like another case file. To create your law firm's website, the following components should be considered:

Clear and Concise Service Descriptions: Ensure that each service your law firm offers is clearly described. Use straightforward language to explain what your law firm does and how it benefits your clients. Avoid jargon and overly technical terms that might confuse your website visitors.

Detailed Practice Areas: Break down your services into specific practice areas. Prospective clients will have the advantage to easily navigate your website based on their specific needs. Each practice area should have its own dedicated section on your website, with detailed descriptions and relevant information.

Professional Profiles: Create individual profiles for each lawyer at your law firm. Include their educational background, professional experience, areas of specialization, and any notable achievements. Professional photos can also help personalize these profiles and make them more engaging.

Mission and Objectives: Clearly state the mission and objectives of your law firm. This helps potential clients understand your firm's values and what drives your practice. A strong mission statement can differentiate your law firm from your competitors and resonate with clients on a personal level.

Client Testimonials: Testimonials from satisfied clients can be included in your Google review and on your website to provide real feedback that can reinforce your law firm's expertise. These elements can help build trust and demonstrate the real-world impact of your services.

Easy Navigation: Your website can be a simple design but, most importantly, it should be easy to navigate. A clean, professional design can enhance user experience and make it easier for your web visitors to find the information they need. Consider using a responsive design that works well on both desktop and mobile devices.

Contact: Your law firm's contact information and contact form for inquiries should be included to serve as a call to action. Where you choose to include a chat box on your website, it is good practice to include an automated message to welcome the web visitors and provide your response time. The purpose of a website is to advertise your services and to enable prospective clients to schedule a consultation with your firm in a manner that nurtures the growth of your business.

Website Updates: Updating your website regularly will boost your law firm's brand. Regular blog posts, legal highlights, or news updates can help to improve the search engine optimization of your website on various search engines, such a Google and Bing, and provide further insights about your practice to prospective clients.

A professional website may sometimes be the first impression a potential client has of your law firm and the set up does not have to be overly expensive. There are various resources that can guide and assist you in building a professional website on a budget such as Wix and Wordpress. The above components can assist you in developing an effective online presence for your law firm to support client acquisition and business growth.

VI.

Value-Driven Content Marketing Strategy.

To strategically position your law firm in the industry, your content marketing strategy should focus on creating informative content that addresses the current legal challenges faced by individuals and businesses. There are various ways to adopt this approach including but not limited to the following:

Blog Posts: Regularly publish blog posts that discuss recent legal developments, completed court cases, and practical advice related to your practice areas. These will showcase your law firm as an authority in these areas, which can attract potential leads to your law firm.

White Papers and E-Books: Develop in-depth white papers and e-books that explore complex legal issues in detail. These resources can be used to educate potential clients and demonstrate your law firm's expertise.

Webinars and Online Seminars: Social media such as LinkedIn has a provision for hosting live webinars. Choosing to host live webinars on current legal issues allows you to connect with prospective clients, which reinforces your law firm's brand and establishes you as an authority in your areas of practice.

Newsletters: Send out regular newsletters that highlight recent legal news, give updates about your law firm, and note upcoming events. This type of regular communication keeps your audience informed and engaged with your law firm.

Social Media Content: Share informative and engaging content on social media platforms. This can include short articles, infographics, and videos that address common legal questions and issues.

Client Testimonials: Showcase client testimonials that highlight your law firm's successes. This builds credibility and demonstrates the real-world impact of your services.

Legal Guides and FAQs: Create comprehensive legal guides and frequently asked questions (FAQs) that address common legal issues and questions. These resources can help potential clients understand their legal options and the services your law firm offers.

By focusing on these content marketing strategies, you can effectively position your law firm as a trusted advisor and attract prospective clients who are seeking solutions to their legal challenges. It will be prudent to include a blanket disclaimer in all of your content to avoid the misrepresentation of the client-lawyer relationship with your audience. Your content should also state that you are not providing legal advice but only legal information.

VII.

Advertising Investment and Digital Engagement Strategy.

Effective advertisement and a comprehensive digital engagement strategy is crucial for the success of your law firm's marketing efforts. Your law firm should focus on using targeted keywords that are relevant to your areas of practice. This ensures that your advertisements reach individuals who are actively searching for legal services related to your expertise. For instance, if your law firm specializes in business law and immigration law, keywords like "business legal services", "commercial law" or "immigration lawyer" should be incorporated into your advertisement campaigns. A structured advertising and digital engagement strategy for your law firm will focus on the following:

1. Advertisement Types
There are several types of advertisements that your law firm can utilize to maximize reach and engagement:

Search Engine Advertisement: These are advertisements that are affiliated to specific key words. Google and Bing are examples of search engines that are effective for capturing potential clients who are actively seeking legal services.

Advertisement on Social Media: There are numerous social media platforms you may choose to use for your law firm's social media advertising. LinkedIn, Facebook, X (formerly Twitter) and Instagram appears to be very effective and quite popular among law firms because they offer targeted advertisement to reach your specific audience profile and demographics.

Video Advertisements: Video content can be highly engaging and is particularly effective on platforms like Instagram and YouTube. These advertisements can exhibit your law firm's expertise and provide valuable information to your targeted prospective clients.

2. Platform Selection.

Choosing the right social media platforms is essential for reaching your targeted prospective clients and maximizing your law firm's digital engagement. The following social media platforms can be considered for your law firm's marketing:

LinkedIn: This platform is quite conservative, and it allows you to network with other professionals in various industries. A business and personal LinkedIn page is essential to establish your law firm's brand in the legal industry. This may either be done in a conservative or creative manner.

Instagram: This platform is exceptional at reaching a younger demographic. There are various ways that your law firm can use Instagram to share legal content and update clients about your services and the latest changes in the law that your firm specializes in.

Facebook: Facebook offers extensive targeting options based on its vast user base. You can enhance your law firm's brand and reach specific demographics, interests, and behaviours. Facebook is also effective for retargeting visitors who have previously engaged with your website.

X (Formerly Twitter): X can be used to share news, and legal updates, and to participate in industry conversations.

3. Content Strategy.

Creating valuable and relevant content is key to engaging your audience and building your law firm's online presence.

The following content type may be helpful in elevating your online presence:

Legal Updates: Share the latest developments in your practice areas. This keeps your audience informed and strategically positions your law firm as a reliable source of legal information.

Client Testimonials: Prospective clients build confidence in your law firm's services based on positive feedback from the firm's previous clients. It is imperative to highlight these clients' testimonials on your website and share them on Instagram as Insta graphics or Insta videos.

Legal Concepts: Educate your audience on complex legal topics. Break down legal concepts into elementary content, such as blog posts, infographics, or short videos.

Team Spotlight: Include the expertise and achievements of your team. This can include professional biographies, interviews, and articles written by team members.

4. Posting Schedule.

Consistency is crucial for maintaining an active online presence. Develop a realistic posting schedule that you can adhere to, such as the following:

Weekly: Post at least once a week on each platform to keep your audience engaged and keep your firm top of mind among your audience. This can include a mix of the content types mentioned above.

Twice a Week: For platforms like X (formerly Twitter) and Instagram, consider posting twice a week to maintain a higher level of engagement. This frequency helps keep your content fresh and relevant.

Resources such as Zoho Social or Hootsuite can assist with your advertisement planning and scheduling.

5. Budget Optimization.

Advertising can quickly become expensive, so you should have a well-defined budget and optimize your spending across various platforms. If you will be managing your law firm's advertisement budget, you should start with a nominal amount before scaling up. This method will ensure that you learn and understand the advertising process. Here are some tips for budget optimization:

Set Clear Goals: Define what you want to achieve with your advertising campaigns, whether it's increasing brand awareness, generating leads, or driving traffic to your website. Clear goals will help you allocate your budget more effectively.

Allocate the Budget across Platforms: Distribute your budget across different platforms based on their performance and your target audience. For example, if LinkedIn advertisements are generating more leads than

Facebook advertisements, consider allocating more of the budget to LinkedIn.

Monitor Advertisement Performance: Monitor advertisement performance across your selected social media as this will assist you with prioritizing your advertising budget, spending, and media of focus to maximize the desired results.

Adjust Your Advertisement Campaign: Adjust your posting frequency and advertisement campaign across your social media based on your advertisement performance and your advertisement metrics. If certain types of content perform better on specific days or times, adjust your schedule accordingly.

Refine Your Content: Feedback and performance metrics can determine the extent of adjustment your advertisement content will require. Attempt using various content presentations to see what suits your audience the best and then adjust accordingly.

6. Audience Targeting and Retargeting.

Effective audience targeting and retargeting are essential for maximizing the impact of your advertisements. Your audience can be based on the following:

Jurisdiction and Demographics: Focus your advertisements on specific jurisdictions where your law firm operates. For example, to yield better results, a small law firm will likely target its advertisements on a specific state, province or city where they can reach the targeted demographics who could use the firm's legal services.

Interest Targeting: If an individual has shown interest in legal services or has visited legal websites, they are more likely to engage with your advertisements. As such, your advertisements can be streamlined to target individuals based on their online interests.

Retargeting: Retargeting advertisements reminds previous visitors to your website of the legal services your law firm offers. This can also prompt these visitors to take action to meet their legal needs.

A detailed digital engagement and advertising plan is essential to effectively manage your law firm's online presence and achieve your marketing goals. By focusing on advertisement targeting, selecting the right social media platforms, creating valuable content, and optimizing your budget, you can build a strong digital presence that attracts and retains clients in the long term.

VIII.

Email Outreach Strategy.

An effective email outreach strategy is essential for nurturing leads, reinforcing your brand, keeping clients informed, and exhibiting your law firm's expertise. A structured approach can help you achieve these goals and ensure that your communications are both impactful and professional. You should ensure that your email outreach strategy complies with relevant anti-spam legislation and include an easy way for recipients to unsubscribe from your emails if they choose to do so. You should also include a clear call-to-action to make it easy for recipients to take the next steps. Below are tips to developing a successful email outreach strategy for your law firm:

1. Client Communication Updates.

Keeping clients updated on relevant legislation and legal developments is crucial for maintaining their trust and confidence in your law firm. Regular communication updates can include the following:

Legal Changes: Inform clients about new laws or amendments that may affect their cases. Provide clear explanations of how these changes impact their legal situation and what steps they should take.

Case-Specific Updates: Regularly send personalized updates to clients about the progress of their case, upcoming deadlines, and any important developments. This helps clients stay informed and feel reassured.

2. Legal Information Email Series.

Creating an email series focused on legal topics relevant to your practice areas can educate and engage your audience. For example, certain practice areas have laws and policies that are constantly updated, such as immigration laws. This can present an avenue to develop a lasting series. Other ways to provide updates to clients or prospective clients can include:

Educational Content: Share articles that explain complex legal concepts in an elementary manner to position your law firm as an experienced specialist in the legal area.

Completed Court Cases: Highlight your successful cases and how your law firm handled them. This demonstrates your expertise and provides real-world examples of your law firm's capabilities.

Commonly Asked Questions: Address common questions and concerns related to your practice areas. This can help potential clients understand their legal options and the services you offer.

3. Monthly Newsletters.

A monthly newsletter is an excellent way to keep your audience informed about current legal issues and your law firm's activities. Your newsletter can include:

Legal News: Summarize recent legal developments and their implications. This keeps your audience informed about important changes in the legal landscape.

Law Firm Updates: Share news about your law firm, such as new hires, awards, or community involvement. This helps build a personal connection with your audience who may, in the long run, decide to engage your law firm.

Insights and Analysis: Provide brief insights and analysis on relevant legal issues. This illustrates your law firm's proficiency and leadership in the firm's practice areas.

4. Automated Appointment Reminders.

For ongoing clients, automated appointment reminders can help ensure that they stay on track with their legal matters. These reminders can include:

Appointment Details: Send reminders with the date, time, and location of upcoming appointments. Include any necessary preparation instructions.

Follow-Up Actions: Remind clients of any follow-up actions they need to take before their appointment. This helps ensure that meetings are productive and efficient.

5. Automated Follow-Up Emails.

Automated follow-up emails are essential for nurturing leads and converting prospective clients who have shown interest in your services. These emails can include:

Thank-You Notes: Send a thank-you email to individuals who have provided their email address or attended a consultation. Express your appreciation for their interest in your law firm.

Additional Information: Provide additional information about your services, such as e-brochures or links to relevant blog posts. This helps potential clients learn more about your law firm.

6. Mobile Adaptation.

To ensure the success of your email outreach strategy, make sure your emails are personalized to the recipient's name and are optimized for mobile devices. Many recipients read their emails on their smart devices, so it is important that your content is easy to read, navigate on smaller screens, and has compelling subject lines.

A methodical email outreach strategy can significantly enhance your law firm's ability to keep clients updated, nurture leads, reinforce your brand, and emphasize your expertise. By focusing on client communication updates, legal information email series, monthly newsletters, automated appointment reminders, and automated follow-up emails, you can create a comprehensive and effective email outreach plan. There are various resources that can help you draft and write your emails as well as generate ideas for blog posts, including but not limited to OpenAI, Grammarly, and ProWriting Aid. Implementing best practices such as personalization, segmentation, and mobile optimization will further enhance the impact of your email communications.

IX.

Client Acquisition Strategy.

Your law firm's client acquisition strategy can leverage both direct and indirect approaches to onboard and retain clients. An effective strategy will focus on relationship building as we have discussed in earlier sections and incorporate various methods to attract and engage prospective clients. Here are some tips to consider:

Inbound Marketing.

Inbound marketing is an effective tool for attracting prospective clients by providing valuable content that addresses their needs and interests. This can be achieved through:

Blog Posts: Regularly publishing blog posts on your law firm's website can help establish your firm's expertise in your practice areas. Topics should be relevant to your practice areas and your clients' concerns, and provide insights into their legal issues, which can drive traffic to your website.

Webinars: Hosting webinars on topics related to your practice areas can engage potential clients and provide them with valuable information. Webinars offer an interactive platform where you can share your knowledge, answer questions, and build trust with your audience.

Referral Programs and Strategic Partnerships.

Building a network of referral sources and strategic partners can significantly enhance your client acquisition efforts. Here are some tips to consider:

Formal Referral Programs: Establishing a formal referral program can incentivize professional contacts and existing clients through discounts. You should, however, review your law society's rules on referrals and incentives.

Mutual Referral Programs: Depending on your areas of practice, consider partnering with professionals in various industries, such as financial advisors and real estate agents, who may refer clients to your law firm. In return, you can refer clients to their services, creating a mutually beneficial professional relationship.

Targeted Outreach.

Targeted outreach can be an effective way to connect with potential clients and introduce them to your services. Consider using the following methods:

LinkedIn: Use LinkedIn to identify and connect with potential clients and referral sources. Share relevant content, participate in discussions, and engage with your network to build relationships and increase your visibility.

Email Campaigns: In addition to the content the about email outreach strategy discussed in the earlier section, you should develop targeted email campaigns to reach potential clients. Personalize your messages to address their specific needs and highlight how your services can benefit them. Regularly update your email list to ensure you are reaching the right audience.

Free Consultation

Offering a limited free consultation can provide immediate value to prospective clients and demonstrate your expertise. This approach allows you to:

Assess Client Needs: During the consultation, you can assess the client's legal needs and provide initial advice. This helps build trust and demonstrate that you are genuinely interested in helping them.

Demonstrate Your Expertise: Use the consultation to highlight your knowledge and experience in the relevant practice area. Providing valuable insights during the consultation can leave a positive impression and increase the likelihood of the client choosing to work with your law firm.

Community Engagement.

Your community and areas of practice can substantially determine the type of events you can host to build community engagement. These events provide an opportunity to share your expertise, answer questions, and connect with potential clients in a more personal setting.

Being visible and active in your community can help build your law firm's reputation and attract new clients.

A detailed client acquisition strategy for your law firm should leverage both direct and indirect approaches to attract and retain clients. Focusing on relationship building and incorporating strategies such as inbound marketing, referral programs, targeted outreach, free consultations, and community engagement can contribute to effectively growing your client base and establish your law firm as a trusted advisor in your practice areas. The key to successful client acquisition is to provide value, build trust, and maintain consistent engagement with your potential clients.

X.

Networking and Mentorship.

Expanding a law firm's network is crucial for attracting potential clients and fostering professional growth. Networking opportunities should be strategically selected to align with your law firm's practice areas. For instance, if your law firm specializes in business law and immigration law, attending relevant events such as an immigration law summit or a relevant business event can significantly enhance your visibility and strengthen your connections within these fields.

Importance of Networking for Law Firms.

Networking is a vital component of business development for law firms. It allows you to build relationships with prospective clients, referral sources, and other professionals in various industries. By expanding your network, you gain deeper insight about current trends in law, and you increase your law firm's visibility, credibility, and opportunities for collaboration.

Types of Networking Opportunities.

To maximize the benefits of networking, it is essential to attend events that are relevant to your practice areas. While you are encouraged to outline the networking opportunities relevant to your areas of practice, below are examples of some key types of networking opportunities that can be particularly beneficial to law firms specializing in business law and immigration law:

Legal and Corporate Law Conferences: These events bring together legal professionals, corporate executives, and industry experts to discuss the latest developments in corporate law. Attending these conferences can help you stay updated on legal trends, regulatory changes, and best practices. It also provides an opportunity to connect with potential clients and referral sources who may need legal services in corporate law.

Business and Entrepreneurship Networking Events: These events are ideal for connecting with entrepreneurs, business owners, and investors. By attending these events, you can showcase your expertise in business law and offer legal solutions to help businesses navigate legal challenges. Networking with entrepreneurs can lead to new client engagements and opportunities to provide legal counsel for startups and growing businesses.

Immigration-Focused Conferences and Expos: These events are specifically designed for professionals working in the field of immigration law. They provide a platform to discuss immigration policies, legal challenges, and best practices. Attending these conferences can help you stay informed about the latest developments in immigration law and connect with prospective clients who need legal assistance with immigration matters or colleagues who may be future sources of business collaboration.

Chamber of Commerce and Industry-Specific Events: Local chambers of commerce and industry-specific organizations often host networking events, seminars, and workshops that present rare opportunities to connect with various industry professionals in the same setting. By participating in these events, you can demonstrate your law firm's commitment to the local business community and build relationships with key stakeholders.

Continuing Professional Development (CPD) Events: CPD events are essential for keeping your legal knowledge and skills up to date. They provide opportunities to learn from industry experts, gain new insights, and enhance your professional development. Networking with other legal professionals at CPD events can also lead to valuable connections and potential collaborations.

Strategies for Effective Networking.

To make the most of networking opportunities, it is important to approach them strategically to ensure the desired outcome. Below are some suggestions to consider:

Your Objective: Your aim for attending any networking event should be clear because this will inform how you focus your efforts to make meaningful connections. Networking events are great for learning about industry trends and meeting potential clients and referral sources. Leaving a potential client with a complimentary card may be getting outdated, however, it is a good idea to have them available in case the opportunity comes up and it seems appropriate to offer a physical or digital complimentary card.

Impact Statement: Your impact statement is a succinct and clear introduction of your law firm's areas of expertise and services. You should always have prepared a concise pitch that highlights your law firm's unique value proposition and practice areas. This will help you introduce yourself and your firm confidently and make a strong first impression.

Engage in Meaningful Conversations: Networking is not just about handing out business cards or eating the foods. Engage in meaningful conversations with other attendees. Ask intelligent questions, be an active listener, be slow to speak and show genuine interest in the work they do. Building rapport and establishing trust are key to forming lasting professional relationships.

Leverage Social Media: Connect with contacts you made through online social media platforms such as LinkedIn to stay connected with your network and share updates about your law firm's activities and achievements. You may choose to connect with your contacts during or after the events. Engaging with your network online can help reinforce your professional relationships and keep your law firm top of mind.

Participate in Panel Discussions and Presentations: If possible, seek opportunities to speak at conferences, CPDs, and events. Participating in panel discussions or giving presentations can position you as an expert in your field and increase your visibility within the industry.

Professional Associations: Networking opportunities are never in short supply when you actively become a member of professional associations related to your practice areas. You will have the opportunity to connect with other professionals through various forums and events organized by these associations.

Expanding your law firm's network is essential for attracting potential clients and staying competitive in the legal industry. Whether you specialize in business law, immigration law, or any other practice area, strategic networking can significantly contribute to your law firm's growth and success.

Mentorship

In the legal profession, it is often said that a junior lawyer cannot thrive in isolation. Beyond networking, mentorship plays a pivotal role, offering invaluable insights from the experiences of seasoned lawyers who have navigated the path before you. A mentor acts as an informal guardian, guiding you through your legal journey, advocating for you within your firm and the industry. You can meet your mentor through professional networks, referrals, or online.

Benefits of Mentorship

The advantages of having a professional mentor are numerous including but not limited to:

Networking: Every mentor expands your professional network which can be a rich source of referrals.

Life Lessons: Gleaning life lessons from your mentor can help you avoid common pitfalls.

Professional Goals: Mentors help you stay aligned with your professional objectives, thereby fostering your professional growth.

Personal Development: Mentors can identify your strengths and weaknesses and guide you in leveraging your weaknesses as potential strengths. thereby enhancing your personal development.

Rules of Etiquette for Meeting with a Mentor.

Mentors especially in the legal profession, offer their time as unpaid volunteers and, as such, a mentor's time and schedule are precious. When you choose to engage with a mentor, follow the unspoken rules listed below.

Professionalism: Maintain professionalism in all interactions with your mentor.

Punctuality: Respect your mentor's time and schedule, making punctuality a priority.

Preparation: Prepare your talking points before each meeting to ensure productive discussions.

TMI: Sharing too much information (TMI) about your personal life tend to put-off mentors. Remember that your mentor is a professional guide, not a personal friend, so avoid sharing too much information about yourself.

Thank-You Note: Cultivate the habit of sending a thank-you email after every meeting to express your gratitude.

It is most beneficial to have a mentor within your area of practice or in a field you aspire to transition into, as this will better prepare you for future challenges. When you benefit from the wisdom of those who came before you, it is equally important to pay this mentorship forward, providing guidance and support to junior lawyers who require guidance. This cycle of mentorship not only strengthens individual careers but also enriches the legal profession as a whole.

APPENDICES.

Marketing Resources

Consider these effective tools to enhance your law firm's marketing strategy:

Website

GoDaddy Website Builder (godaddy.com/website-builder)

Jimdo (jimdo.com)

Squarespace (squarespace.com)

Weebly (weebly.com)

Wix (wix.com)

WordPress (wordpress.com)

Zyro (zyro.com)

Search Engine Optimization (SEO)

Ahrefs (ahrefs.com)

Answer the Public (answerthepublic.com)

Google Analytics (analytics.google.com)

Google Search Console (search.google.com/search-console)

Moz Pro (moz.com)

SEMrush (semrush.com)

Yoast SEO (yoast.com)

Email Marketing

AWeber (aweber.com)

Constant Contact (constantcontact.com)

GetResponse (retresponse.com)

Hubspot (hubspot.com)

Mailchimp (mailchimp.com)

Moosend (moosend.com)

Social Media Management

Buffer (buffer.com)

CoSchedule (coshedule.com)

Hootsuite (hootsuite.com)

Later (later.com)

Loomly (loomly.com)

Sendible (sendible.com)

Zoho Social (zoho.com/social)

Advertisement

AdRoll (adroll.com)

Bing (ads.microsoft.com)

Facebook Ads (business.facebook.com)

Google Ads (ads.google.com)

Instagram (facebook.com/business/ads/Instagram)

LinkedIn (linkedin.com/ads)

Social Media Platforms

Meta (facebook.com)

Instagram (Instagram.com)

LinkedIn (linkedin.com)

Twitter (twitter.com)

Practice and Client Management

AbacusLaw (abacusnext.com)

Clio (clio.com)

Cosmolex (cosmolex.com)

LEAP (leap365.ca)

MyCase (mycase.com)

PracticePanther (practicepanther.com)

ULaw (ulaw.io)

Artificial Intelligence

ChatGPT [OpenAI] (chat.openai.com)

QuillBot (quillbot.com)

Writesonic (writesonic.com)

Jasper AI (jasper.ai)

Grammar

Grammarly (grammarly.com)

ProWritingAid (prowritingaid.com)

LanguageTool (languagetool.org)

Hemingway Editor (hemingwayapp.com)

Linguix (linguix.com)

TARGET PROFILE EXAMPLES

Industry-Specific Profile Example

Client Profile: Real Estate Broker

Name: Mustafa Oshodi

Age: 60 years

Job Title: Real Estate Broker

Company: Olan Brokerage Team

Location: Toronto, Mississauga, Brampton ON

Industry: Real Estate

Annual Revenue: $275 million in transaction volume

Clients: High-net-worth individuals, property investors, and commercial real estate clients

Experience: 35 years in real estate brokerage, specializing in luxury residential and commercial properties

Goals

Close High-Value Deals Smoothly: Olan Brokerage Team's

primary goal is to close complex and high-value transactions for their clients while ensuring all legal aspects are handled efficiently. Olan Brokerage Team works with both sellers and buyers, needing legal support on both sides.

Manage Client Risks: Whether a multi-million-dollar residential sale or a commercial property acquisition, Olan Brokerage Team's clients depend on them to minimize their risks, particularly with complex contracts and legal issues.

Expand Portfolio: Olan Brokerage Team is constantly seeking to grow their real estate business and need to ensure that they have the right legal support to handle large, complicated deals involving long-term leases, joint ventures, and partnerships.

Compliance with Real Estate Regulations: As a broker firm working in Ontario's highly regulated market, Olan Brokerage Team must ensure that all transactions comply with local real estate laws, zoning regulations, and fair housing practices.

Challenges

Complex Contracts: Real estate transactions, especially for commercial properties, involve complex contracts that need to be suited to specific deals. Olan Brokerage Team often negotiates on behalf of their clients and require legal assistance to ensure contracts are well drafted.

Client Due Diligence: Olan Brokerage Team frequently works with investors and buyers who require thorough due diligence, including title searches, property liens, and ensuring zoning compliance. Handling these legal elements efficiently is crucial to securing deals.

Litigation Risks: Disputes between buyers and sellers, or issues arising from unclear contract terms, can lead to litigation. Olan Brokerage Team needs to work with a law firm that can preemptively resolve legal issues before they escalate.

Motivations

Reputation and Client Retention: Olan Brokerage Team's business depends on maintaining a stellar reputation for closing high-value deals and providing excellent service.

Ensuring smooth legal processes helps build trust with her clients and secure repeat business.

Client Satisfaction: Olan Brokerage Team's clients expect top-tier service, including legal expertise that can streamline the buying or selling process. Quick, efficient legal solutions are key to satisfying their clients, especially in competitive and high-pressure markets.

Time-Efficiency: Real estate transactions, especially in hot markets like Ontario, require fast turnaround times. Delays in legal processes can cause deals to fall through, so Olan Brokerage Team values legal partners who can work quickly and thoroughly.

Legal Needs

Contract Drafting and Review: Olan Brokerage Team deals with numerous contracts, including purchase agreements, commercial leases, and partnership agreements. They need legal support to draft, review, and negotiate these contracts to protect their clients' interests.

Due Diligence and Title Searches: For both residential and commercial transactions, Olan Brokerage Team's clients rely on them to ensure that all due diligence is completed, including verifying property titles, identifying liens, and ensuring proper zoning.

Litigation Support: When deals go wrong, Olan Brokerage Team needs a law firm that can provide litigation support and protect their interest, whether its disputes over contract terms, commission issues, or buyer-seller conflicts.

Regulatory Compliance: With Ontario's strict real estate regulations, including zoning laws and fair housing regulations, Olan Brokerage Team needs ongoing legal guidance to ensure their transactions comply with local laws.

Objections to Hiring a Law Firm

Cost Sensitivity: Although Olan Brokerage Team works with high-value clients, they need to manage costs to ensure that legal fees do not substantially decrease their commissions. They prefer law firms that offer transparent pricing or package services.

Perception of Speed: Delays in legal services can cause deals to fall through or prolong transactions. Olan Brokerage Team value law firms that can work quickly, handle urgent matters, and prioritize their deals.

Communication Issues: Olan Brokerage Team require regular updates and clear communication from legal teams. They often work in high-pressure environments where a lack of timely communication can result in missed opportunities or frustrated clients.

How Alpha Zero Law Firm Can Help

Specialized Real Estate Expertise: Alpha Zero law firm offers deep expertise in both residential and commercial real estate law, providing Olan Brokerage Team with the assurance that their clients are protected in every transaction.

Responsive Legal Service: Alpha zero law firm prioritizes quick turnarounds for time-sensitive deals and offers personalized legal solutions that fit the fast-paced nature of Ontario's real estate market.

Comprehensive Legal Packages: Alpha zero law firm provides flexible billing options, such as flat-fee services for contract review or bundled services for large transactions, ensuring Olan Brokerage Team can manage costs effectively.

Proactive Legal Guidance: By offering proactive legal advice, Alpha zero law firm will help Olan Brokerage Team stay ahead of potential issues, such as regulatory changes, title complications, or contract disputes.

Generic Client Profile Example

Client Profile: Small Business Owner

Name: Tinu Dade

Age: 42

Job Title: Owner & CEO

Company: Mukaka Restaurants Inc.

Location: Toronto/GTA

Industry: Food & Beverage (Café/Restaurant)

Annual Revenue: $1.5 million

Team Size: 15 employees

Stage: Growth (expanding from one location to multiple)

Goals

Expand the Business: Tinu Dade plans to open two new locations within the next few months and needs help with securing leases, franchise agreements, and zoning compliance for her new stores.

Hire and Manage Staff: With the expansion, Tinu Dade is hiring more employees and needs to ensure that their employment contracts, policies, and compliance with labour and employment laws are up to date.

Protect the Brand: As their business grows, Tinu Dade wants to ensure their branding, including her company name and logo, is legally protected through trademarks and copyrights.

Minimize Legal Risks: Tinu Dade is concerned about avoiding lawsuits from employees, customers, or landlords and wants to ensure her business is legally protected from liabilities.

Navigate Commercial Real Estate: Tinu Dade needs help with negotiating and reviewing commercial lease agreements for her new locations to ensure favorable terms and avoid future disputes.

Challenges

Limited Legal Knowledge: Tinu Dade has been managing legal matters independently, but she recognize that her expertise is limited. She is unsure about the legal nuances of expanding her business and feels overwhelmed by the complexity of legal contracts and compliance issues.

Budget Constraints: As a small business owner, Tinu Dade is conscious of costs and worries about expensive legal fees. She needs a law firm that can offer affordable, transparent pricing without compromising on service quality.

Employee Issues: As her workforce grows, managing employee-related legal issues such as compliance with wage and hour laws, anti-discrimination policies, and employee benefits has become increasingly complex.

Contract Complexity: Negotiating contracts with suppliers, landlords, and potential partners is becoming more frequent, and the business needs help understanding and negotiating these agreements to avoid potential disputes.

Motivations

Business Growth and Sustainability: Tinu Dade is driven by the desire to grow her business successfully without legal missteps that could derail her expansion plans. She wants a strong legal foundation to protect her brand and operations as her business scales.

Risk Management: Tinu Dade is aware of the risks involved in running a small business, especially as it expands. She wants to mitigate these risks by ensuring all legal matters, from employee contracts to property leases, are properly managed.

Long-Term Success: Beyond just expanding, she wants her business to be legally sound for the long term. She is motivated to create a sustainable business model that can withstand potential legal challenges and protect her personal assets from liabilities.

Legal Needs

Business Structuring and Compliance: Tinu Dade needs legal advice on structuring her business properly, whether it is creating a new corporation for the expanded locations or updating their existing corporate structure to meet legal requirements.

Employment Law: As she hires more staff, Tinu Dade needs to ensure her business complies with employment laws, including wage and hour regulations, employee rights, and proper employment contracts. She also needs help creating employee handbooks and non-compete agreements.

Contract Drafting and Negotiation: Tinu Dade regularly negotiates contracts with suppliers, landlords, and contractors. She needs legal support to review, draft, and negotiate these agreements to protect her interests and avoid future disputes.

Commercial Real Estate: As Tinu Dade business expands into new locations, she requires legal expertise in commercial real estate to negotiate favorable lease terms and ensure compliance with local zoning and permitting laws.

Intellectual Property Protection: Tinu Dade wants to protect her brand, including her logo, business name, and proprietary recipes, by securing trademarks and patents to prevent infringement by competitors.

Objections to Hiring a Law Firm

Cost Sensitivity: As a small business owner, Tinu Dade is highly sensitive to legal costs. She needs a law firm that offers flexible pricing structures, such as flat fees or affordable retainer options, to avoid unexpected costs.

Perceived Complexity: Tinu Dade is wary of hiring a law firm because she feels the legal process might be too complicated and intimidating. She needs a law firm that can simplify legal matters and provide clear, actionable guidance.

Time Efficiency: Tinu Dade values her time and does not want legal matters to slow down her business operations. She needs a law firm that can provide quick turnarounds on legal work without sacrificing quality.

How Alpha Zero Law Firm Can Help

Affordable Legal Services: Alpha zero law firm offers flexible pricing models, such as flat fees for certain services and cost-effective legal packages for small businesses, making it easier for Tinu Dade to manage her legal budget.

Specialized Expertise: With experience in business law, employment law, and commercial real estate, Alpha zero law firm provides comprehensive legal support that addresses all of Tinu Dade business needs as her business expands.

Proactive Legal Advice: Alpha zero law firm will help Tinu Dade stay ahead of potential legal issues by offering proactive advice on structuring his business, complying with employment laws, and protecting her brand.

Quick Turnaround and Responsive Service: Alpha zero law firm prioritizes responsiveness, ensuring that Tinu Dade receives timely legal guidance without unnecessary delays.